zendoodle coloring

Naughty Puppy

Other great books in the series

zendoodle coloring

zendoodle coloring

Naughty Puppy

Mischievous Mutts to Color and Display

illustrations by

Deborah Muller

CASTLE POINT BOOKS

NEW YORK

ZENDOODLE COLORING: NAUGHTY PUPPY.
Copyright © 2020 by St. Martin's Press. All rights reserved.
Printed in the United States of America. For information, address
St. Martin's Press, 120 Broadway, New York, NY 10271.

www.castlepointbooks.com

The Castle Point Books trademark is owned by Castle Point Publishing, LLC.
Castle Point books are published and distributed by St. Martin's Press.

ISBN 978-1-250-25355-2 (trade paperback)

Our books may be purchased in bulk for promotional, educational, or business use.
Please contact your local bookseller or the Macmillan Corporate and Premium
Sales Department at 1-800-221-7945, extension 5442, or by email
at MacmillanSpecialMarkets@macmillan.com.

First Edition: February 2020

10 9 8 7 6 5 4 3 2 1

FRENCH FRIES

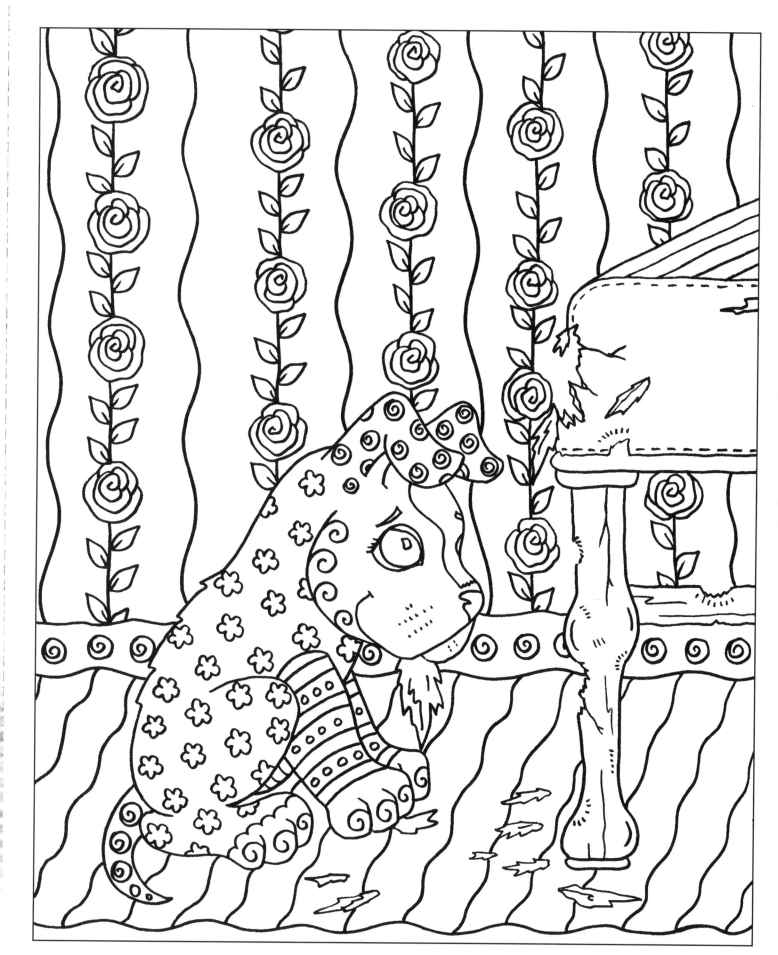